Safari Sam's Wild Animals

Polar Animals

W

FRANKLIN WATTS

LONDON•SYDNEY

Franklin Watts
First published in Great Britain in 2015 by The Watts Publishing Group

Designed and illustrated by David West

Dewey number 591.7586
HB ISBN 978 1 4451 4498 6

Printed in Malaysia

Franklin Watts
An imprint of
Hachette Children's Group
Part of The Watts Publishing Group
Carmelite House
50 Victoria Embankment
London EC4Y 0DZ

An Hachette UK Company
www.hachette.co.uk

www.franklinwatts.co.uk

SAFARI SAM'S WILD ANIMALS POLAR ANIMALS
was produced for Franklin Watts by
David West Children's Books, 6 Princeton Court, 55 Felsham Road, London SW15 1AZ

Safari Sam says:
I will tell you something
more about the animal.

Learn what this animal eats.

Where in the world is the animal found?

Its size is revealed!

What animal group is it – mammal, bird, reptile, amphibian, insect, or something else?

Interesting facts.

Contents

Arctic foxes eat lemmings, voles, ringed seal pups, fish, seabirds and birds' eggs. They also eat berries and seaweed when available.

Arctic foxes live throughout the Arctic region.

The Arctic fox grows to around one metre long from head to tail.

Arctic foxes are members of the mammal family. Mammals typically have fur or hair and give birth to live young.

In winter, when there is little **prey** around, Arctic foxes will follow a polar bear to eat the leftover scraps from its kills.

Arctic fox

Arctic Foxes

The **Arctic** fox is a hardy animal. It has short ears, a short nose, furry soles to its feet and a thick fur coat to keep it warm in freezing Arctic temperatures. Its coat is white in winter and turns brown or grey during the summer so that it is well **camouflaged** in all seasons.

Safari Sam says:
The Arctic fox can survive in freezing temperatures of -50°C. This is very cold. A kitchen freezer is -18°C.

Safari Sam says:
Travelling from one place to another over long distances is known as migration in the animal world. The Arctic tern has the longest regular migration of any known animal.

Arctic tern

Arctic Terns

The Arctic tern is one of the most travelled of all birds. It spends summer in the Arctic and as the temperatures become cooler it flies south. It arrives in the **Antarctic** in time for the summer months there. It travels there and back in the same year, a distance of 71,300 kilometres.

Arctic terns eat small fish or crustaceans. Sometimes they may eat berries and insects.

It is found in cooler parts of North America and Eurasia during the northern summer. During the southern summer it is at sea, reaching the northern edge of the Antarctic ice.

Arctic terns have a length of 38 centimetres and a wingspan of 76 centimetres.

Arctic terns are members of the bird family. All birds have feathers and lay eggs.

The average Arctic tern travels 1.6 million kilometres in its lifetime.

Caribou

Caribou live in the cold Arctic regions. Their special coat keeps them warm. It has two layers of fur – a dense, woolly undercoat and a longer-haired overcoat made of hollow, air-filled hairs. Their noses are specially adapted so that the cold air can be warmed up when they breathe in.

Safari Sam says:
Caribou have large hooves that are big enough to support the animal on snow and to paddle through water. Their hooves have sharp edges to grip on ice.

Caribou

Caribou mainly eat **lichens** in winter and the leaves of willows and birches, as well as grasses, in summer.

Caribou are found in the northern regions of North America, Europe, Asia and Greenland.

Caribou grow up to 2.1 metres in length.

Caribou are members of the hoofed family of mammals.

Some Arctic peoples farm herds of semi-wild caribou for their meat, hides, antlers, milk and for transportation.

9

Killer Whales

Killer whales are the largest of the dolphins and one of the most powerful **predators** in the ocean. They hunt in family groups, called pods, of up to 40 individuals. They can grab seals from the ice with jaws crammed with teeth that are 10.2 centimetres long.

Safari Sam says:
Killer whales are intelligent and have been seen teaching their young hunting skills.

Killer whale

Killer whales eat seals, sea lions and even whales. They also eat fish, squid, penguins and other seabirds.

Although they often live in cold waters, killer whales can be found from the polar regions to the Equator.

Killer whales grow up to 9.1 metres in length.

Killer whales are members of the dolphin family of mammals.

Killer whales are also known as the orca whale or orca.

Musk oxen

Musk oxen live in the frozen Arctic. Their long, shaggy coats are well adapted to the freezing Arctic temperatures. In winter they use their hooves to dig through snow to graze on roots, mosses and lichens.

Safari Sam says:
When threatened by wolves, musk oxen form a circle, each facing outwards, with their young in the middle.

Musk ox

Musk oxen eat grasses, Arctic willows, woody plants, lichens and mosses.

Musk oxen live in the Canadian Arctic and Greenland. Small populations have been introduced in Sweden, Siberia, Norway and Alaska.

Musk oxen grow to 1.5 metres high at the shoulder.

Musk oxen are members of the mammal family.

The outer hairs of a musk ox, called guard hairs, cover a second, shorter undercoat that provides extra **insulation** in winter.

13

Narwhal

Safari Sam says:
Narwhals make some of the deepest
dives ever recorded for sea mammals,
diving to at least 800 metres.

14

Narwhals

Narwhals are known as the unicorns of the sea. They have two teeth. In the males one tooth grows through the upper lip into a spiral tusk. Sometimes narwhals rub their tusks together in an activity called tusking.

Narwhals feed on fish, shrimps, squid and cuttlefish.

The narwhal is found mainly in the Atlantic and Russian parts of the Arctic Ocean.

Narwhals can grow up to 6.1 metres long. Their tusks can grow to 2.7 metres long.

Narwhals are members of the porpoise family of mammals.

Narwhals use **echolocation** to find prey and to detect obstacles in murky water.

Penguins

Penguins are flightless birds that have adapted to life in the water. Their wings have become flippers. They spend about half of their time in the oceans. They have a thick layer of feathers that keeps them warm in water.

Safari Sam says:
Penguins that live in the Antarctic huddle together to escape the icy wind and to keep warm. Each bird takes turns moving into the group's protected and warmer middle.

Penguins feed on fish, squid and krill.

 Penguins live only in the southern hemisphere, especially in Antarctica.

 King penguins are the second largest of all penguins. An average bird stands about one metre tall.

 Penguins are members of the bird family.

 King penguins keep their newly laid eggs warm by balancing them on their feet and covering them with their feathered skin, which is known as a brood pouch.

King penguins

17

Polar bears live mainly off seals but have been known to eat musk oxen, caribou, birds, eggs, rodents, crabs and other polar bears.

Polar bears live within the Arctic Circle, which includes the Arctic Ocean, its surrounding seas and surrounding land masses of Eurasia and North America.

Polar bears can grow up to 2.4 metres long.

Polar bears are members of the mammal family.

Polar bears are very strong swimmers and have been seen swimming hundreds of kilometres from land.

Polar bear cub

18

Polar Bears

Polar bears have a thick coat of insulated fur, which covers a warming layer of fat. They spend many months of the year roaming the sea ice, hunting their favourite food, seals.

Safari Sam says:
The colour of a polar bear's coat provides camouflage in the snowy environment. Under their fur they have black skin, which helps to attract the warming rays of the Sun.

Walrus

Walruses eat shrimps, crabs, tube worms, soft corals, sea cucumbers and various molluscs – especially clams.

Walruses live in the Arctic around Greenland, Canada, Alaska and parts of Russia.

Walruses grow up to 3.4 metres long and can weigh up to 1.4 metric tons.

Walruses are members of the mammal family and are closely related to seals.

Walruses use their tusks to haul their bodies out of the water and to break breathing holes into the ice from below.

20

Walruses

These massive sea mammals are often seen lying on ice floes with hundreds of others. They have thick skin over a thicker layer of fat, called blubber. The males have large tusks and bristles on their snouts.

Safari Sam says:
Walruses use their sensitive bristles to find clams and other seafood in the murky waters on the sea floor.

21

Wolves

Wolves live and hunt in packs of around six to ten animals. They are very social animals and **cooperate** with each other to bring down large prey, such as bison. They have very dense and fluffy winter fur, with short underfur and long overcoat hairs.

 Wolves hunt large animals such as caribou, elk, moose, bison and musk oxen. They also eat small mammals, birds, fish, lizards, snakes and fruit.

 Wolves are found in Asia, Greenland, small parts of Europe and North America, with many living in the Arctic.

 Wolves can grow to more than 1.5 metres long from head to tail.

 Wolves are members of the dog family of mammals.

 Wolf packs have large territories and are known to roam large distances – as much as 20 kilometres in a single day.

Grey wolf

Safari Sam says:
Wolves are best known for their spine-tingling howl. Howling is their way of talking to each other over long distances.

23

Glossary

Antarctic
The region at the South Pole.

Arctic
The region at the North Pole.

camouflage
Colour or patterns on an animal that help it to blend in with its surroundings.

cooperate
To act together as a group.

echolocation
The way some animals 'see'. They emit sounds that bounce off objects.

insulation
Usually a layer of material that keeps a body protected from heat or cold.

lichen
A simple plant that grows on rocks, walls and trees.

predator
An animal that hunts other animals for food.

prey
An animal hunted for food.

Index

24